IAN GOUGE -
SELECTED POEMS: 1976-2022

ⓑ

Other Books by Ian Gouge

Novels and Novellas

On Parliament Hill - Coverstory books, 2021
A Pattern of Sorts - Coverstory books, 2020
The Opposite of Remembering - Coverstory books, 2020
At Maunston Quay - Coverstory books, 2019
An Infinity of Mirrors - Coverstory books, 2018 (2nd ed.)
The Big Frog Theory - Coverstory books, 2018 (2nd ed.)
Losing Moby Dick and Other Stories - Coverstory books, 2017

Short Stories

Degrees of Separation - Coverstory books, 2018
Secrets & Wisdom - Paperback, 2017

Poetry

The Homelessness of a Child - Coverstory books, 2021
The Myths of Native Trees - Coverstory books, 2020
First-time Visions of Earth from Space - Coverstory books, 2019
After the Rehearsals - Coverstory books, 2018
Punctuations from History - Coverstory books, 2018
Human Archaeology - Paperback, 2017
Collected Poems (1979-2016) - KDP, 2017

Anthologies

Making Marks in the Sand - Coverstory books, 2022
New Contexts: 1 - Coverstory books, 2021
Triple Measures - Ian Gouge, K.M.Miller, Tom Furniss, Coverstory books, 2020
Oak Tree Alchemy - Coverstory books, 2019
Play for Three Hands - Tom Furniss, Ian Gouge, K.M.Miller, pamphlet 1981

Non-Fiction

Shrapnel from a Writing Life - Coverstory books, 2022

IAN GOUGE
SELECTED POEMS:
1976-2022

Completely Revised

First published in paperback format by
Coverstory books, 2022

ISBN 978-1-7397660-6-1

Copyright © Ian Gouge 2022

www.iangouge.com

www.coverstorybooks.com

Contents

Previously Unpublished

✿

Foreword

At a recent reading event, I was asked which of my collections was my 'best book'. It was an innocent enough question, designed to aid a purchasing decision. It was also an unfair question. Any marginal preference I may have for one or the other is inevitably dwarfed by the knowledge that there are good pieces in all my volumes of poetry and that, in expressing a preference, a potential reader will always be in danger of missing out on something I would like to think 'worthy'. Yet you can't expect your average reader to buy all your books!

For a while I had been toying with the idea of pulling together a 'selected works', gathering all my favourite poems under a single cover. This notion had been growing in strength partly as a result of more regular attendance of 'open mics' at which I sometimes struggled to decide what to read; wouldn't it be rewarding to be able to take a single book to such events knowing every piece inside was a live candidate? On the back of that ambition, the 'best book' question only added fuel to the fire.

So here it is, a 'Greatest Hits' from my seven collections published to-date. And, because I couldn't help myself, I have thrown in a small number of as yet unseen poems. Of course, I should also say that this endeavour in no way diminishes the value of the individual books themselves; there are many more poems that might easily have found their way into this volume had size not been a consideration.

Perhaps they're for a 'complete works' at some point in the future..!

Ian Gouge
May 2022

COLLECTED POEMS: 1979-2016

Cormorants Diving

I stood on the sea-wall
and watched cormorants diving
into the cold grey sea,
you nearby
- watching me watching them -
knowing I had not seen you
nor spotted your sophisticated
remote control device.
You fooled me with your body
and its language -
and as you fooled me then,
so the cormorants rise
always where I did not expect to see them.

Cormorants diving, you say,
is a simple matter of being able
to hold your breath under water.

From the Lighthouse

So that was it,
the journey of a lifetime,
resolution of the myth.
There was no romance
only solitude in the echoes
on the dark stone stairway;
only discomfort in the harsh salt-spray.
Who could want this disappointment,
the looking back over the shoulder
at nothing in particular?

Perhaps it's only here we attain
some understanding
of the soaring of a gull
upon the grey-white winds,
between the lighthouse and the land.

Perhaps.

But who can explain
why unsaved ships still blindly steer
onto waiting rocks?

If it were no more than dream
the lighthouse would be gone,
our search for meaning satisfied,
the intrusion relieved.
Looking back over the shoulder
at nothing in particular,
the lighthouse is there still.

It was a Party

It was a party
and in the dark
I asked your name,
saw your face illuminated by garden lights.
As we danced I held your hand.

Then stooping,
from the grass I raised
a fragment
and presented it to you:
"a piece of my broken heart
to wear on your dress".

It was a party
and in the dark
you went into the house to examine my gift,
to look disappointedly
at that given you:
"no heart at all
but a piece of broken glass".

M ourning

The day promised fair;
a valley awoken by sun
into Spring initiation.

From rough-trod paths
a burst of colour
sequestered in a knot of shadow:
forget-me-nots,
love-lies-bleeding.

Coincidence might have joined them
but for his hesitation,
as if he caught in her eye,
in her attitude, in the way
she stooped to pick the flowers,
a silent warning;
her hand outstretched,
the flowers resting there,
love-lies-bleeding,
forget-me-nots.

Separate Journeys

Somewhere I have a photograph of her
sitting on a low wall outside a railway station
legs frozen in mid-kick at nothing;
and there, at her feet,
the evidence of another Oxford Street sortie.

For all her confidence and that air of stability
she seemed always to be travelling -
from one place to another or between friends.
She was rooted of course, but elsewhere,
in the omnipresent God that divided us;
of that part of her, I could grasp nothing.
Even then I could see her fading away,
unable to accept an embrace
on my terms, without qualification.
She said I made her feel free
yet never knowing at what cost to me.

That was an age ago, and even her words
"I shall never desert you" have lost their force.

Before our separate journeys
- different discoveries for different reasons -
there was both nothing and everything between us.
Perhaps that is the paradox of love.

Somewhere I have a photograph of her
sitting on a low wall outside a railway station.

Shakespeare

"And what does Shakespeare mean to you?"

Softly-stubbled fourteen year olds stumble
over 'the quality of mercy';
awkward, wrong-sexed Portias
who'd rather be playing football or
spraying graffiti on railway cutting walls -

places they can be more articulate.

Skipton

The dales were flooded.
At the top, snow on the ground,
ice in the cracks of the dry stone wall;
below, in remorseless cold,
Skipton
grey and grim.
All that way
and still the big hills in the distance,
still in the sun.

Evensong time;
the uneven peel of church bells against the hills
spilling into the flooded fields.

S t Ives
(for W.H.Auden)

Were you here, struggling for context,
you might concede how things change -
or not changing, how they are fixed:

sons like fathers; daughters, mothers;
a patchwork of forlorn tans,
plastic balls, dark glasses, and bathers

splashing at the edge of an inevitable sea.
You might argue how even this
- from bathing rags to cream teas,

beach towels to broken bottles -
might manufacture a cry
(or at best, some feeble rattle!)

against what is to come.
Men, too soon grown old, play football
in mimicry of younger days; and sons

(yet to know of their tragedy!)
endure the legends of the Tellers.
Young men - wearing puberty

like some gaudy medallion -
stride the beach, striving for an image
only time and disappointment can bring.

A pulse of caravans brings them South
(along arterial roads, you might have said)
clogging motorways, blocking the mouths

of narrow lanes they cannot navigate.
They arrive over-burdened,
and what they leave behind is opaque;

memory lacking a peg to hang it on.
History is a fading parking ticket;
the remnants of suntan lotion;

tatty books upon the chalet's shelves;
your craggy face in the mirror.
And then we drive away ourselves,

and all the while imagining
the indefinable talent
Old Masters had with suffering.

The Torturer's Horse

The Torturer's horse waits heavy-hoofed
and thinks about pissing.
Somewhere beyond unrefined grey walls
its Master goes about his business,
unheard cries failing to break the silence
of an overcast and gloomy dawn.

Soon they will sleep, for this is their pattern;
to be about during the very last
of the darkest hours and then,
except in the most inclement of times,
trudging the damp lanes home.
It tugs at the grass more from boredom

than hunger, feeling the press of the saddle
as it lifts its head to hear, what?
Perhaps the sliding of a rusted bolt
beyond a solid door; perhaps faint footsteps,
or the slow reluctant grind
of drawbridge chains.

Shaking its head - flies or a vague
desire to stay awake? - the metal noose
to which its reins are tied
bemoans granite captivation,
the fog about the moat almost rendering
the whole scene invisible.

Simultaneously sound and steam rise
from its hot urine, accompany
the sounds of liquid splash on mud,
of metal on granite, of bolts in doors,
and the cries that come
from the breaking of bones.

The Word-Surgeon

The Word-Surgeon
hacks at words with his blunt knife,
dissecting them,
spilling their guts on his grubby table.
Scientifically he is searching
for something undiscovered,
something tangible with which to finally defy
those old-fashioned, irrational theories.

"Humbug!" he says,
knowing precisely the order of the letters,
their relationship, their parentage.
Then tensing his butcher's hands
bloodied by silent consonants,
he plunges again into the heart
of another innocent syllable.

Walking Through Fire

I

A memoir is in progress
despite persistent rumours
that you know your world,
an accidental gathering of people.
Beyond your reach
in an iron mask
lies conquest of the Ancients;
history the hard way.
Your first village
never permanently lost
its place in the sun;
your self-reliance
rooted in rarefied but lonely childhood
- its privilege and curse,
the weight of words.
Friends with a winning technique
go with the tube
that is the company spirit,
while you - suffering by choice
a discovery of vocation -
still sell your time for money,
moving with a generation
in the new spirit of hope,
aware of the possibility of failure.

Are you any more than
an old-time crusader
dying of unnatural causes
yet taking nature seriously?
The legend that is your lifetime
parallels modern art
and realms as yet unopened.
- There is little we can do that is new -
Your high purpose?
To report only what you personally experienced
(and only partly understood),
somehow repaying the debt for
escape from the hospital;
undertaking, against all odds,
a pilgrimage into the future.
A mythic element draws you on
to the art of pure ascent
- We will all die and be forgotten -
and with a protean talent for disguises
you take your proper place:
a casual walk to the blackboard to write

WE ARE PROUD OF THE BIRTHDATES OF OUR CHILDREN.

Water upon rock,
self-inflicted wounds
look like an optical illusion;
making deserts bloom
is a quality of unlost wilderness.
Your sense of the holy
is invigorated by wide spaces
and a burning purity of spirit
vulnerable to grief.
Yet the dignity of the land prevails
and you make a double crossing
with nothing but your own thoughts,
marks, and martinis....

The Magnificent Failure,
fit enough to survive.

After nine years of dreaming
there is no shipwreck saga,
only nuance through fluid gestures
existing for a moment, then lost.
To have given choices
is the achievement of a lifetime
discovered almost by accident.
Seeing is surviving,
so the quest goes on -
for an undiminished man
digging a sculpture garden
or (the ultimate aerial elegance!)
landing on a planet inhabited.
You venture to the very peaks
in search of illusive images:
the lonely sound of a steam whistle;
a flash in a mind's eye;
an old bucket in the jungle;
a monument to knighthood.
You vow to emulate rugged grandeur,
to spearhead a wrinkled radical movement
starting afresh
no matter what the consequence.

Still the lure of Make-Believe,
of walking in the sky
until a morning comes
beyond all limits.
Dawn, a fishing boat;
a moment out of the past.
On a hillside above a village
on which the sun never set,
mountains treated to their own surprise
describe the best route between two points;

a subtle communication,
a gift of the gods
impossible to photograph.

To catch the wind
from a windblown utopia
snug and watertight;
to change something profound,
(the mist off the river
- neither fire nor ice -
picked up at midnight).
Ageless in a dream of Earlyspringtime,
the thrill of victory persists.
A gift for being in touch,
an incredible sense of destiny;
the fate of the maverick to be damned.

II

A culture caught in time
stages open revolt
to fight against impossible odds
for a regeneration of spirit:
- *Change IS possible* -
So the new breed
expeditions in the harsh desert,
as if one needed to doubt their insanity
caught in a thunderstorm on high ground:
weather is so total.

**THE SECRET LIES IN PEOPLE,
THE PRINCIPAL BUSINESS OF MY LIFE.**

Urban pioneers vow to rebuild
a place to belong to;
a pastoralist utopia, a technical fix.
An illiterate and poor juggler
is discovered alone in a cathedral,

a model of ambition and behaviour,
a David knowing that Goliath would fall.
A Samaritan for eagles
savours the thrill of a Mending
- *He can fly!* -
once again wild and free.
And on the street
the juggler dreams of other feats -
the element of the unexpected,
the miracle of balance.
And a real love story
- the only thing you really wanted in the world -
just stands in the centre and grins.

Thinking they could reflect the sun,
legendary nomads rode to freedom
in Civil War with society:
from Refugee to President
- both implausible roles -
the official easy way out.
Some people would die
before the stars collide;
hopefuls battling for right,
trapped in a bad dream
repeated with ritualistic precision.
God, the minimalist actor, does what counts:
the powerful pleasure of a singular man
in the house he grew up in,
raising money to finance his vision
without long-term obligation.
And God, free to feel a conversation
for authenticity in life,
inspires amateurs to sing
of revisions in understanding;
of exceptional things attempted.

Every week for six days
a creature of comfort
dreams in a state of mind
related to a cultural context
and the discipline of another age.

EVERYTHING EVERYBODY LOVES IS THE SAME.

The school for prodigies
too lazy to work
discovers the Scarlet Runner
when all else fails.

III

Existing only to display its own errors,
the puzzle of history
flounders in the pool of plot,
only at the end relaxed
even if the same questions continue to go about.
Deciding against suicide,
crops no-one wanted
represent the only tomorrow.
If no-one sends flowers,
travel from basement to basement,
doomed to perpetual childhood
in the front line.
War usually ends in a tie;
the survival of the whole -
man's will against man's limitations -
a cruel test for a paradise
howling in utter despair.
Grass and sea run at each other,
land dies in cliffs,
and a village is saved from descent into a feeling of history.

Lighter than the spade,
lessons from megalithic men
offer a culture without cities and writing,
teasing out trapped capacities:
a lone hand and arm;
the yellowness of flowers in the mind
(a limited offering, the painted mind!)
stretching the imagination
backward and downward,
signposts clearly lettered.
New T-shirt designs
bring back a dying town
sacrificed to commitment
and a lifetime in the galleys.
And in a case of mistaken identity
imagination becomes an enemy,
the bleakest exercise of the mind,
a dazzling blonde riding shotgun unexpected.

In all history
a sense of perfection
may yet survive,
a chronology of the first apocalyptic days:
the rush to disasters;
incredible artefacts passed from hand to hand;
works destroyed in their appreciation.

THE IMAGE IS SELF-EXPLANATORY AND DOES NOT IMPLY
MORE ABOUT THE VALIDITY OF THE SUBJECT.

Age is no barrier;
still an enigma,
an irreverent homage
to the power of imagination.

Look for a small piece of land
to study trees while cutting:
people swinging an axe
offer a key to the wilderness;
in the fallen tree
is an abstraction of the natural world,
an isolated fragment.
Pursing this nearly forgotten craft
takes its rider through a lifetime
- *I am proud of the birthdates of my children* -
in a game of emotion, not reason,
ever within boundaries of credibility
and a residual sense of isolation.
Oh, the joy of sets;
of walking through fire
to where the words live!

Witches' Point

Plain trees form the ridge-back
of this stunted, inelegant isthmus;
the foreshore - a discarded litter
of stones - changes mistrustingly:
the haphazard scorpion's tail;
a dog crocheted of pebbles;
a winter's fist pointing south.

In the deceiving grey of a photograph
distilled like a memory from childhood,
across the blank face of an even sea
pulls the distant oarsman.

Worthing

Mid-Winter Worthing at dusk
is an old lady getting ready for bed.

Slippers off, she stretches arthritic toes,
pushing at wrinkled stockings with effort,
pushing at years of life's undeniable tides.

Curlers out, her wispy greying hair
mixes elegance with tired beauty,
fragile and vulnerable like an empty shell
on a vast and deserted beach.

Yung Wind

The shadow from the mountains to the ridge
defines the vast extent of his great acreage,
and from atop the barren and infertile col
he pauses (leaning thus against a boundary wall)
and takes into his compass those plantations
- of chestnut, hazel and ting-tree formation -
within which rich and fertile panoply
he finds his comfort.

And thus he sees
assurance and justice in his course,
and with the coming war, the crops' translation into horse.

from The Classic Anthology defined by Confucius (ed. Ezra Pound)
Folk Songs, Book 4
Yung Wind, VI Ting

HUMAN
ARCHAEOLOGY

T he Grand Tour

Flying through a thin light-suffused mist
is the feeling of travelling across centuries
where physical distances have evaporated
and rationality itself might only have a limited hold.
A sun of dull gold rose through tinted windows
and dawned the intimacy of waking up among strangers;
below, a landscape dotted with red-brick buildings
already bathed in fluorescent light and
some vague actressy notion of glamour.
Surfaces cannot be trusted amidst
the spread of modernity whose depth is hard to gauge.

This had been a preparation of sorts.

We had hoped for a blistering morning of soaring white,
yet saw paper kites wheeling against a grey polluted sky;
saw a city that was a world
less colonised, more muscular;
a warren of narrow streets through which arteries had been forced;
an area of heavy boulevards;
a sandy waste delimited by a pale line of trees.
It seemed like grafting the geography of one city onto another,
a temple town staring frankly into the void
with an aloof and scolding memory
both of the heat and the passage of time.

The train had a romantic name, bringing us
to an almost intact medieval life full of pilgrims,
foreigners in their own land
come empty-handed into a less familiar world.
There is always dismay at the first sight of squalor;
flecks of pink in the dark oily water are
plastic bags, like dead jellyfish, small imperishable memorials.
A smoky electric light wafts out

through cloying waves of jasmine
as the evening tide of worshippers sweeps along,
bathers digging at the water with folded hands.
In signs of recognition and curiosity,
tourists photograph the disarray:
the wheeling birds on the river;
a grotesque co-mingling of light and shade;
a place where people come to die.
Strong-faced ascetics watch the scene from their haunches
as the seed of something very old fertilises the present,
an old culture, decaying for centuries
like a scene out of Chaucer.

This had been a pilgrimage of sorts.

Yet there is a new tyranny of borrowed things
- bootleg educational courses and aphrodisiacs -
in an ugly new vitality.
This vision of urban apocalypse reveals
small flyblown towns with foul air,
desolate but for giant advertising boards.
Two poles in a world increasingly divided
where faith functions by an internal logic
in intolerable limbo, its middle condition
a lesson in the fragility of a power
that is bound to be broken.

Spirituality and self-discovery inextricably linked,
the drama of his appearance
and the force of his gaze
betrays the intensity laying coiled within him.
He wanted desperately to be in politics,
to portray the rage of people who knew they were once something;
yet knowledge of old languages proves
an incomplete armoury against a modernity
demanding a new class of interpreters.

This had been a translation of sorts.

The city reappears from the haze,
branches casting long shadows over powder-blue walls
almost as a kind of disguise.
There is uncertainty in rural life;
people crushingly unsure of themselves
are those for whom the past is still alive
wrapped up in the perfume of worship,
the vestiges of grand culture,
and a denial of distinctiveness and originality.
The seasons are no longer on their side.

He is looking for a way out of the nightmare of history,
retreating in the face of rough manners
and trying to salvage a sense of self.
Language, once vivid, has become jargon
in which word and meaning have parted ways,
an ill-fitting garment that muffles the voice,
an impediment to communication.
He betrays a palpable sense of despair
that a great historical event could not
simply be shrugged off as regrettable accident,
a misadventure shrouded in mutual embarrassment.

"Here is the problem of what to do with the past;
there is more to civilisation than endurance."

I was haunted by the memory of a man
using words with a painter's confidence
yet who could not see himself from the outside
even when what mattered was the example of his life.
We lacked a shared vocabulary,
our conversation running into the dead walls
of a language that meant everything to him.

The Grain of the Wood

Do you see that face in the grain of the wood?
The hooked nose; the frown above bushy eyebrows?
Do you sense the menace in that warped smile?
There is witchcraft and entrapment there.
Do you see the wings of that bird,
spread wide in its swoop toward the window,
lured by sunlight and the make-believe of escape?

Perhaps it is mainly children who can see these things;
innocents who see elephants and alligators in clouds
through car widows on long motorway journeys.
Is it the freedom of imagination
or the chains of boredom
that opens their eyes this way?

Do you recall the copse near the lake
where we used to stray an age ago?
And if so, can you see, etched in your mind's eye
the clumsy initials we once carved there?

Since you have been gone
I have not ventured to the lake, that copse;
but somehow, once again, I can see
monsters in the grain of the wood.

The Balloon

Against a uniform grey sky, a balloon
      unexpected in its redness.
Escaped from a party perhaps,
      it floats with purpose
      seemingly ungoverned by the air,

as if steering a course
to where all balloons must gather.
Mesmerised, you watch it for a while
until height and distance make it small,
indistinct, insignificant.
Yet somewhere else, other eyes cast skyward
see the balloon for the first time
and contemplate its origins
and the purpose of its journey.

Perhaps there is a secret place,
magical, mystical,
where all free balloons meet,
where through the blending of their vibrant skins
they cast an arch of multi-coloured light
radiant across uniform grey skies.

E choes

With no pills to drive me to sleep
I learned abandonment in strange hotels
greeting the early morning light,
purple in winter, pink in summer.
So I could absorb more of each place
I tried to marvel at the iron bridge,
to speak English and not think it a foreign language,
sat at cafe corner tables recently abandoned.
Walking through history in a stealthy but solitary line
I sensed ghostly footsteps on the treads
their secrets almost visible in living colour
growing deeper the longer we were away.
They are a lifeline to a world I too often leave behind.

Nostalgia in Black and White

She was good at remembering old movies,
at staring down a gun and pleading for a cigarette
with no way to tell which way it would go.

Sometimes we remembered being happy
and the testing questions to figure out who we were -
pasts so unbelievable we needed a witness for our memories.

Solitary now, avoiding even basic upkeep
in fear of arbitrary self-inflicted punishment,
I could live another's life in the soundtrack's music.

The Permanence of Shrapnel

There is a photograph of the house in
                              an aerial view of an estuary
and on the glass that frames it
                              smudge marks left by museum goers
who have pointed out his former home.

Perhaps reverence comes from knowing
                              genius is so elusive;
rare enough to warrant understanding, investigation.
                              Research triggers ethical concerns.
It is a kind of archaeology where
                              ideas and insights are kindled,
where suggestions and notions fall
                              below the common standard
that might have been expected, considering.

Ignoring vague hypotheses, for him
                              clarity would arise at unexpected times,

the happiest of accidents where
                        promise and opportunity collide
and lead him beyond the confines of his study
                        to words he had no intention of playing
suddenly dredged from the estuary's silt almost,
                        cloaked in layers of muck and magic,
whose smoothing and polishing
                        unravelled complex and mythical qualities.

Yet still he feels like a hopeless casualty,
                        the wounding bullet still in place,
his attempts to self-medicate
                        wedded to the verdict of history
and the smudge marks on a photograph's frame.

E xtra Time

Later, when we searched your room -
dust from freshly-drawn faded curtains
flying abundant in the air as if
independent beings with minds of their own -
we found the sports' things of your youth
hidden in a corner behind a trunk,
its leather cracked and worn.
It had seen better days.
Too pliable to be of use now,
the strings of your racquets were soft
belying the past they must have shared;
you - red-faced, enthusiastic -
chasing down the ball cross-court
to drive a winner down the line
and shout "Advantage!"
I swear I caught a glimpse
in Uncle's normally unwavering eye
the beginning of a tear

waved away with a complaint about the dust
and how you never kept things clean.
Perhaps he knew you better than I;
brother first, father later.
If so, I did not mind.
My memories were elsewhere,
not confined to a room of ancient things
smothered by the dust of years
or the chill illumination from
a sudden winter light.

R ipples

We used to fish in the summer,
hand-held lines disappearing into the rippling lake
invisible after the first foot or so.
We kid ourselves still about the blueness of water
and the perfection of the sky,
but on some unblemished days you could
pick out the ribs of the boat from the shore café
where our parents took tea and scones, and combined
protection with indulgence in our freedom.

Once Jack caught a small silver fish
and we argued over its name
waiting too long to return it to the water,
disappointing the girls with its needless demise.
If there were accidents, I do not recall them now.
I remember laughter and boisterousness,
and once losing an oar over the side,
the boat rocking wildly and generating
fear and fun in equal measure.
If our parents noticed they never said,
rather choosing to softly lecture us on safety
and offer mild admonishment when more than five of us

went out at any one time.
I blur those days now into a single image
- of Jack holding up the fish, the girls laughing,
and somewhere in the bow, me intent on my line
and staring through the water -
an image that has become a photograph,
something stored in my mind to represent
childhood and how it is supposed to be idyllic.

It would be good to go fishing on the lake again,
but we would need two boats now
even though Jack's no longer with us;
his summers numbered all too few
only living on in our memory of them.

A mnesia

Her memory flowed like a movie,
tragedies and humiliations etched most sharply
in the exaggerations our mind creates
during the magic of turning perceptions into memory.

Experiencing the residue of promise or fate,
her extraordinary obsession with her past
was like stepping into a time machine.

But now, trapped in the limbo of an eternal present,
living under a narrow spotlight surrounded by darkness,
every lost thought seems less like a casual slip
and more like droplets of life that immediately evaporate,
fallen completely out of time.
All that lost knowledge was once at her fingertips,
like a culture before the advent of books.

A bstraction

Romance is an overlay on reality;
rose-coloured glasses that filter
what we choose not to see.
What is the past but history
become an abstract we cannot trust?
There can be no history without romance;
the Emperor's new clothes.

We are seduced by facades;
we swallow draughts of romance
and pretend to know the past;
we look at the remarkable and miss the profound;
we take photograph after photograph,
yet capture nothing
merely applying another coat of varnish
that keeps us from the past
 - or protects the past from us.

"Sometimes," said the Photographer,
"I don't take the shot
because the moment is what's important,
and how can you capture that?"

True history resides in all the photographs
that were never taken,
beneath veneers never applied,
like a ghost silently pacing marble halls
sensed but unrecognised.

PUNCTUATIONS FROM HISTORY

Punctuations from History

i

"The loop shares a kinship with
a remnant from the brewhouse"

        scarred by tawny rust
                the imprints of a Cooper's fingertips
                    the aura of oak and hops

        caught in a shaft of sunlight
        a glint from history
        as if illuminated dust might rearrange itself
        to turn back time
                to bring back echoes from the forge
                    the headiness of ale
        come full circle
        even as the loop leans unused   unwanted
                forgotten against the ruined walls

ii

"A chair cut in half but still standing
damaged, halved, surviving"

        split asunder
        mimicking past usefulness
        presenting a fractured image of itself
                nonchalant
                as if nothing had happened
                as if it had always been thus

        a chair that is not a chair
        a thing that is not a thing
                become image   or parody
        disguised to look like itself
                    or how it was

we nod at the deception
and recognise in the once-chair
a mirror of ourselves
and how we were
        or how we are now
                or how we might yet be

iii
"In sympathy with the plight of Saints
a pilgrimage full of geographical detail"

        factual is not spiritual
        full of instruction and order
        of where, or when, or how
                to march
                to eat
                to rest

        the journey is a test
        in fulfilling the rules of adherence

        orienteering without passion
        collecting the badge
                the certificate of completion

        this is about trophy not selflessness
                a tick on a bucket list   not self-discovery
                        closure   not an awakening

iv
"Elongated and tailored to the topography
a spirit level unable to find equilibrium"

        disproving the feeling
                that you are on even ground
        the power of the bubble holds sway

a demonstration of air
     and gravity
          and forces beyond our comprehension

adjusting   re-sighting
     we hope for another outcome
     as if there must be a way
     to disprove this reality

suffocated   unable to escape
     we resign ourselves
     to the uncertainty of imbalance
     and cast the level
          into the tilting skip

v
"The markers of space around language
an ever-present sign of life"

     there is energy in the void
          and unseen potential

     scrabbling in the mottled dark
     with inadequate instruments
     we endeavour to excavate
          our uneven treasures
     hoping when they are cleaned
          polished to a new and burnished hue
     they reveal something undiscovered
          - or at least unseen in our lifetime

     have you noticed how beyond
     Archaeologists' veneer of romance
          their clothes are shabby
          and their skin scarred
          like the earth in which they dig?

Theft

Their faces were stolen in 1828
when stained-glass lead outweighed
the souls of people.
Empty spaces now stare back,
the blank ovals leave no clue
to the characters of Saints who
unknowingly made the sacrifice.

Two centuries of loss are commemorated
by collages in a sculpture exhibition;
shadows and whispers from the past
and a brief note in the simple catalogue:
"their faces were stolen in 1828".

seen in Haddon Hall, Derbyshire [13th August, 2017]

Changing Faces

i. The Mask

Look.
A largely forgotten cultural artefact
fundamental to notions of identity,
to effacement, disguise, and the resonance
of hiding motivation and concealing truth;
the mask has greater significance
than would first appear,
its duality revealing the way
the world is viewed by both
wearer and audience,
the change into some other being

an absolute separation
of the everyday self.

Complexity and subtlety of meaning
are integral parts of a masquerade,
an event, a performance;
the entire ensemble
implicit in cunning trickery,
the suspension of belief
transforming identity.

Only those who were privileged
had the right to own ancestral masks,
could afford the impersonation of character
to create an indeterminate nature
at the boundaries of interaction between
truth and falsehood,
the human and the spiritual,
the living and the dead.
Masks inhabited by forefathers,
shadows of their former selves,
offered the dream of ancestral return.

Masks, it could be said, carry memory.

Metaphors for the moments of change
observed behind glass-fronted cabinets,
reduced to their sculptural essentials,
masks in museums stripped of their
extra-human dimension and idealised identity
are just a display of dead things.

ii Mask of a Young Woman

Whitened with eggshell,
hair and feathers delicately painted on;
the false eyebrows high on the forehead
and the blackened teeth
fashionable cosmetic styles for over a thousand years.

Theatre masks provided opportunity for expression,
standard masks for different dramas
where subtle changes of expression were honed
by the way in which the head was turned.

iii In the Form of a Wolf

Clan headdresses were worn at feasts by native peoples,
headdresses of cedar bark and goat wool,
regalia to celebrate life-cycle events.

A member of the eagle clan
came across a wolf smiling,
something stuck between his teeth.
The mask removed, the wolf disappeared
only to reappear again in a dream.

Regalia was passed down the female line.

iv Mummy Mask

A depiction of the head and chest
was worn outside the shroud
to act as a substitute for the head
should it become lost;
the spirit could leave the confines of a tomb
and when returning recognise its host.
Created from layers of wet linen

moulded over a thin outer skin,
mummy masks were rarely portraits,
their backs decorated with a row of deities
and seven short columns of near intelligible hieroglyphs.

v Death Mask of Oliver Cromwell

Used as a model for posthumous portraits
here was a permanent record of the way he looked
captured before the features started to fail
(his wart succumbed to the embalming fluid!).

Later his body was exhumed
and his real head displayed on a pole
to be finally buried in Cambridge in the 1960s
300 years after he died.

Subsequently the Death Mask was sold many times.

vi Mask of a Demon

In Life, a significant event
was an attack by
one of the eighteen disease demons.
A primitive antibody
used in healing rituals,
the most powerful of cures was a masked performance
of both dramatic moments and comedy.

vii Wooden Face Mask

Distended cheeks were associated with the city,
the ruler blowing blessings onto his people.

> [And the meaning today?
> Being bloated, or the expulsion of air in relief,
> as if to say "I got away with that one"…]

viii Wooden Helmet Mask

Representative of an ideal of female beauty:
glossy skin,
small facial features,
folds of fat at the neck.

During initiation
girls were kept in check
and masks used to regulate female behaviour.

Apart from this exception
masking traditions were
activities otherwise limited to males.

ix Stone Funerary Mask

Sculpted in a greenish stone
selected for its symbolic value,
these were heavy masks
not intended to be worn
but rather mounted on a wooden armature
and dressed with elaborate costumes.

Inheriting subtle elements
from earlier traditions,
the features of this funerary mask

and the symmetry in its surface
echoed rigid architectural canons
and public mythologies of the ceremonial.

x Cavalry Sports Helmet

Resplendent,
the richly-decorated equipment
- beaten brass shining golden yellow
embossed with battle scenes -
was worn on cavalry sports events,
flamboyant displays involving complex manoeuvres.

The youthful lively faces of the soldiers
a contrast to the chilling, immobile faces of the masks.

xi Yam Mask

Decorated yams were
exchanged between men
and displayed publicly,
the ancestral spirits represented
feted with offerings and decorations
to seek spiritual well-being and
survival in a single cosmology.

Cocktails in the Infinity Pool

Singapore wears her skirts high above the knee,
proud of her slim and tanned thighs.
Her shopping malls mesmerise,
their glimmer, gold and glitz, veneer-deep,
a skin of tropical sweat glistening
on a body we all desire.

Across a polished sky, a grey mass
threatens to unload its burden;
rain that will sing as it bounces off
swimming pools and Ferraris,
trapping you where you stand
or forcing you indoors,
into air-conditioned boutiques,
French pastries, Italian coffee and
faux New York sidewalks.

And yet.
There is history here if you care to look,
if you bother to make the journey out to Kranji
or see Changi as more than just a destination
for departures and duty-free;
long hauls of another kind are buried
not so far beneath the surface.
Perhaps it is apt that her history
is a precious metal to be stroked not scratched,
to be caressed by cotton gloves
and melancholic remembrance
- and then forgotten,
conquered by expeditions to Channel, Louis Vuitton,
and cocktails in the infinity pool.

On Finding Themselves In Darkness

On finding themselves in darkness
they tried to speak eloquently of the stars
and conveyed surprise at their number,
brightness, brilliance,
            or that they were there at all.

It was a lesson in the inadequacy of language
watching them struggle to portray
the mix of wonder and awe that probably
chased their breath away
            and left them smaller than before.

They should lay in a hammock
loose-strung between two acacia trees
and stare upwards from the African scrub
where pollution of the sky cowers
            beyond the furthest horizon.

They should merge that sense of the infinite
with the loneliness of being cast
adrift in thousands of unvarnished acres
accompanied by barks and howls and sounds
            beyond your comprehension.

This indigo vastness is close-coupled
with a finite that can only shrink,
with a worthlessness that can only grow,
with a pulse that is suddenly becalmed
            even as the heart skips a little.

C oast

Trace around its outline with great care,
there is danger as well as beauty there.
Go slowly, cautiously;
try to picture postcard scenes
of secluded coves, a deserted beach,
the caves where smugglers hid
and waited for the tide to reach.
Pause again where once upon a kid
you ate fish and chips with Gran,

or cream fruit scones with Auntie Fran;
or walking that neglected path,
held hands with Ruth's sister, Cath.
Crab fishing from the pier!
Or chasing pollock with a plastic reel;
a Fair, a Carousel, the Dodgems' cheer,
Candy-floss's sickly smell,
screaming at the Waltzer's spell;
a litany of buckets, spades,
vampires, Goths, Sunday parades,
yachts, hovercraft, Bank Holiday swathes
of tourists, row boats, crazy golf,
and over-flowing ice cream sundaes.
You touched the sea more than you knew.
Retracing steam to Dartmouth,
the winding roads to Lyme, St. Ives;
coach trips near and far,
Saltburn's red funicular;
Blackpool's lights, Brighton's sights,
Bournemouth nights, and Whitby frights;
a multicoloured film of wooden huts,
of dunes and skimming stones,
castles of sand fighting incoming tides;
of grit in shoes when walking home
dodging dog shit, the ends of fags,
of wading in the freezing drink
which made your little willie shrink!
Trace your finger round the coast with care;
where land meets sea, your history is there.

F ragments

The uneven planes of a shattered mirror.
A conversation only partly overheard.
The remnants of a broken plate.

Images lost or ill-defined
marry shapes and edges for
memory's trial, a virtual jigsaw.

Was it really sunny that day?
Was the train on time or late?
Did I plan it all so well,
or did I leave it all to fate?

Seven years' bad luck?
An inflection missed?
Did that plate escape wet hands?

The lure of flawed hindsight,
to know if - spoken or thrown in anger -
outcomes betrayed how we felt.

Did it rain ceaselessly,
closing all the sea-front stalls
as we, close-coupled in a shelter,
watched waves assault the sea-front walls?

Here is the mark of absence where it hung.
The phone has gone; the line is dead.
Dust balls circle the once-swept floor.

We close our eyes to open our minds,
sifting through fragments
for the missing piece.

Was sea-fret the reason
I lost you on the front that day?
Or were there other clues - a mirror, a plate -
as to why you went away?

The Light of Our Lives

We have a jar in our bedroom
where we keep the fragment
that fell from the sky and
buried itself in the garden the day
we moved into our new house.
Some days the shard would glow
and the jar illuminate
with an impossible light,
and if we removed the lid
the light escaped and our world
and our lives became
just a little more wonderful.
We were blessed when it landed.

But recently the glow is more reticent;
our rock is alive less frequently
and it has become harder to top-up
our lives with this astral gift
and we are forced to carry on
as if it never arrived,
as if we were just like other people.
Each evening before bed
I check the jar, ever-hoping;
wishing once again to be able to let
a fraction of the brilliance escape.
But it is always dark these days
and when the lights are off
our bedroom is as black as the sky.

Reflection in a Cracked Mirror

I know the Earth in an intimate way,
        our addiction to time and
the systems that keep us alive.

Today is taken up with one long task:
        the looking back to see where we failed.
And so I try to put myself in their place,

to re-learn that doubt is worse than hunger,
        is the offspring of the myopic,
is a fatal threat the closer it gets.

Life is not haphazard,
        even if we're blinded by the
stunning contrast from light to dark

where the whole of humanity,
        cast adrift from truth, is
in need of a chance to heal.

We lose each other easily,
        denying our duty, succumbing to the
rhythm marking time for a few short hours.

Greybeard's Lament

Sitting in the cafe of an up-market supermarket
retired couples make intermittent small-talk,
all light rain-jackets, pseudo-fleeces and 'Bags for Life'.
Blending into one, their faces an amalgam
where none are different.
Yet hey have charted unplanned journeys

through ungovernable seas
like medieval explorers, faces full to the wind,
Captains astride the decks of their ships.

But that is too romantic,
too far-fetched for a damp Tuesday morning
somewhere in the North of England.

Dangerously relaxed with fruit scones,
I avoid the mirror
and slouch deeper into the settee's corner
to practice
                        cultivation.
I strive to be more Pirate than Captain,
feint an illusion to spring, vigour unbridled,
cutlass brandished, steel flashing,
readiness unquestioned.

Eyeing me suspiciously
Doreen clears used plates and cups clatteringly
as if to say
            "Who are you kidding?"
            Crumbs and detritus hold us back
            as do questions about the weather
            and Two-For-One special offers.

Burt Lancaster appears at my side
- or doesn't really as he's unseen by Doreen -
and says
            "Who are you kidding?!
            I was the 'Real Deal',
            from here to eternity…
            Or as close as."

The extent of *my* gymnastics
is bounded by the 'i' crossword
and minor triumphs over harder Sudoku.

They're victories of sorts
when sipping tea and eating scones
in a supermarket cafe on
a damp Northern Tuesday.

A utumn

the church bells were ringing
their evensong peel
yet how could you hear them
an invisible wind stealing
the sound away and sending it
cascading across the open fields
like a broken promise

AFTER THE REHEARSALS

J ukebox

Someone once told him
                    there were two reasons for everything.
He liked to think it would have been Jess,
the Jess he hadn't seen for so long now.

Eyes closed.

It was an effort to get this far.

The doctors told him he was doing well;
recital of their standard patter.
Reason one: to make him feel better.
Reason two: to make them feel better.
The theory seemed to stand up to scrutiny.

He'd come to cherish these rare drug-induced lucid moments.
His medication offered perhaps two brief daily windows
into his past, his life;
if he were lucky, there might be three.
If he were *really* lucky they'd upgrade the dose.

Once upon a time he had been unstoppable
          - whatever that meant.

The drugs allowed him to recreate himself,
to walk again the streets of Sienna or Split,
to take the train all the way to Basel.

From somewhere indistinct yet strangely familiar,
an image of the Styx Ferryman.
He tried to wave it away with a fluttering of his eyelashes.

Two reasons.
It seemed like a new idea, but it couldn't possibly be so;
a universe, one way in, two ways out?

Starved of music,
this old jukebox could only play the records inside it;
the discs were fragments of his past.

All he could do was slide an imaginary coin into the machine
and see what played next.

Suddenly it felt like heaven.

C hristmas in Ambleside

At the last minute
they managed to find a minuscule cottage to rent,
crammed into the middle of a small Ambleside terrace,
and when the weather allowed
spent days wrapped-up against bitter winds
walking the hills.
In the evenings they huddled by the fire,
watched re-runs of old movies on the ageing television
and struggled with inadequate wi-fi.
They told each other it didn't matter.
It was 'romantic'.
Without saying as much,
they placed apostrophes around the word.

Although he had no idea what it was supposed to feel like -
Christmas, their intimacy, their unspoken routines,
even the way she seemed to know when he needed coffee
or just some time to himself to read -
it felt like growing up,
as if that was how adults were supposed to behave.

Coming Together

Opening the door, she found him
    shrunken, lost, defeated,
and "Poor Mags"
    was the first thing she said.

Then she pulled him in
    as much with her force of will
as the arms that enveloped him,
    that begged him to be still.

Comfort the first thing to offer,
    rousing him, bringing him round,
the rescue of a beached sailor
    whose ship, running aground,

he had abandoned; his life
    left to the fate of the mistress sea,
his body battered, his hopes
    in the wreckage of memory.

A Fair Exchange

I hold the world but as the world, Gratiano,
A stage where every man must play a part,
And mine a sad one.

shakespeare   you know what to expect don't you
even if you hadn't read   or seen any
almost as if it were gifted   imbued into your psyche
part of your dna   your life force
the quality of mercy   and all that shit

Tell me where is fancy bred,
Or in the heart or in the head?

that was how it felt   suddenly off-balance
side-swiped by an experience that was   well
almost out-of-body   as it were
he struggled   not knowing where this newness
fitted in the grand scheme of things   in his history

But love is blind, and lovers cannot see
The pretty follies that themselves commit.

it wasn't as if he'd been   on the lookout
or anything   it wasn't as if he thought himself ready
to go back into battle   to fight for glory
he hadn't forgotten the last war   nor cleared
the battlefield   of all the mines

What, wouldst thou have a serpent sting thee twice?

it was fitting   considering shakespeare and the merchant
that it felt transactional   like a commercial contract
he might have said mercenary   if he'd thought of it
but he didn't   anyway he wasn't ready
to play the romantic   wasn't seeking a portia

Must I hold a candle to my shames?

she'd known where to find him   in the market of the mind
you might say   a tradesman in others' ideas
librarian of everything   owner of nothing
and if no words were exchanged   as opposed to the silver
in sealing the deal   the arrangement was plain enough

It blesseth him that gives and him that takes.

it suited them both   she wasn't perfect after all
nor trying to be so   neither did she want any more
than he was prepared to give   that was her gift
releasing him from any bond   not wanting a pound of flesh
just his flesh   and all of it

No longer the smell of small miracles

Supposed to be antiseptic white
the ward had a shade about it, shadowed
by the years of comings and goings
as if each unimportant journey
left something of the traveller behind.
In spite of the off-ness of its colour
- or the colour it possessed
where there should have been none -
it smelled just as it should:

       harsh white linens
       ointments
       discarded newspapers
       old coffee cups
       new flowers in new water
       old flowers in old
       bandages
       cleanliness.

For most it was the smell of endeavour,
of hope, of luck, of trust;
it was the smell of small miracles.
For Jess, staring at the unmade bed,
it was the smell of death.

Knowing her father had made his contribution
to defeat the whiteness of the room,
she picked up his shallow little bag   and left.

For the Love of Daffodils

Expecting tradition,
expecting a smothering of black,
        of sorrowful faces,
expecting the epitome of dirge
        (whatever that meant)
she was surprised by how people smiled,
by how vibrant they looked.
Everywhere was yellow and orange and white.
It had been his request,
to remind him of his garden;   he said,
people should dress as if he were there
        and to celebrate daffodils
                his favourite flower.

She had never known that.

They had entered serenaded by Cat Stevens, of all people:

> "It's not time to make a change,
> just relax, take it easy,
> you're still young
> that's not your fault,
> there's so much you have to know."

'Father and Son', a song for both the Absent and her.

She cried.

> "I was once like you are now,
> and I know that it's not easy,
> to be calm when you've found
> something going on."

At the lectern, sharp and clean as if it were
designed for a business conference,
a man in a suit went through the motions,
reading his script, talking to the delegates
about a man he didn't know.

For a moment she was angry.

Then another man, her father's age,
dark suit, white hair, bright yellow tie, stood up,
standing to the side as if not wishing to intrude,
knowing he was a supporting act.
He looked at them,
                        at the heavy coffin,
and betrayed by his red eyes,
looked down at the sheet of paper
shaking in his hands, and said

      "I have a message from Douglas."

✿

You all look lovely.   It's like spring has sprung all over again!
Thank you.   I wish I could be there with you - though I am of
course, in a manner of speaking.   Did they play the Cat Stevens?
Something for Mac and Jess, though not very original, I admit.   I
hope you made it back, Mac.   If not, know that I'm thinking about
you - which I realise is a little bit the wrong way round, but there
you have it.   Our lives encapsulated.   If I were a religious man -
no, that's wrong.   If I were a 'believer' then I'd make some smug
comment about being on 'the last journey', knowing that there is one
final, glorious, never-ending tour-stop where the gin & tonic never
runs out and Chantilly cream and pickled onions are banished!
But I'm not, and so - with due regard to my few believer friends - I
know I'm not going anywhere any more.   At least not consciously.
Which is actually fine, isn't it?   Inevitable, but fine.   I've had, as
they say, a fair crack at it; life.   There are some things I am proud
of, most of which are, in one way or another, represented by the

people here today.   Look around.   Smile.   If anything, remember
that each one of you here is part of my story, made up part of my
story.   Made me.   So don't let that part of you, or anything I had
to do with *your* story, slip into the fiery furnace.   Never let those
things go.   They are precious, unique, ours.   I gift them to you, for
you to keep, to look after.   Treasure them.   Please.

❈

After, people bequeathed stories of his humour, his honesty,
the practical jokes he played when he was younger.
There were tales of bravery too.
She hadn't known he had rescued a boy from drowning,
diving into the Avon fully clothed
downstream from Worcester.

"He didn't like to boast about it" her mother said.

And she wondered how much folklore
had been lost to her through his modesty;
and she wondered how much she knew him after all.
Replaying the song in her head -

>   *"All the times that I've cried*
>   *keeping all the things I knew inside*
>   *it's hard, but it's harder to ignore it."*

- she cried again.

---

 hoice

Sometimes there is a choice.
Not stark or binary, like heads or tails
where outcomes are known
            even if their consequences are not;

but subtle, nuanced,
flavoured like the addition of herbs and spices
to raw ingredients,
the Magician's trick to serve up
Italian, or French, or Asian.
The essence is not in 'yes' or 'no'
but how the judgement is delivered, embellished,
the tone of voice, the careful wrapping of an answer
bound in patterned paper,
tied by a ribbon that has been teased
until it curls professionally.

Or not.

Not because there is no smoothing,
no way or need to coat the pill;
but because - beyond the camouflage of self-deceit -
the choice *is* yes or no, heads or tails,
its core undeniable, its ripples
on an infinite journey to unseen shores.

FIRST-TIME VISIONS OF EARTH FROM SPACE

First-time Visions of Earth from Space

Sailing in an endless star-studded sea
they tried to find words to convey their new reality.

Knowing a single image can never be all the story,
they were subject to an irrepressible desire
to record this improbable oasis.

Constrained by meaning and connotation
words are fault-full when searching for ways to describe blue.

Experiments with Words

"We initially found them hopping around in a lab,
homely & ungainly & quite ordinary,
behaviours written into genes like automatons
- though that may not be the perfect analogy.

"Later, we set them free, trying
to get a clear picture of their wanderings,
giving them no choice but to travel
- both the escaping and the coming back.
Being able to experiment like this
simply underscores how far we've come!"

Striving to be first to decipher a jumble of datasets,
we explore output in unprecedented detail
stressing ourselves over lattes and amaretti
and creating complex algorithms for calculators
- a nail-biter because the battery was failing.

Cubism & Picasso

On the wall, tightly imprisoned by right angles,
the painting commands attention.
Shapely arms clasp a patchwork
of incomplete and incoherent images,
splintered perspectives working voraciously
to lay bare the imperfection of the world we live in;
fragmented, obscure and discrete shards become whole,
the unveiling of clues for ticking off a checklist.

Endowed with courage and vision,
 driven by obsession and dedication,
  such qualities tainted relationships
   and over-worked them to a muddy ochre.
    Life at the circus, death at the bullfights,
     and Art, the only things he was interested in;
      and Art, the only thing he was;
       and Art, the only thing.

Greatness reveres the ones who commit to the process,
          who offer in two dimensions an illusion of depth,
                 the ability to renew the world constantly
                      and embody the inflection points
                           in our culture.

Civilisations collide in unbounded curiosity / revitalised by
brushstrokes, puffs of / colours merging on a gritty canvas. /
Immersed in the clutter of exuberant minds / we focus inward to
access our feelings, / to reassemble from their vision / our
understanding of a shattered world.

Passion

where did it go
slipping like rainwater through
cracks   in   the   pavement
a deluge
fated to remain nothing   but a memory
a tale to be retold over tea and scones
as if we were just old friends
catching up
not people who were once
      caught out
          by the rain

The Cut-out

I try and imagine the irregular space he will leave,
the awkwardness of it. Will it have boundaries,
soft-boiled edges prone to compromise if you're careless
like stranger-bumping in a Tesco's chiller aisle?
Stolen from unconcerned history and devoid of value
I could take this abstract replica in all its coarse dimensions
and prop it tottering where he stood
to see if he's still at home in 'The Oak', the bookmakers,
the empty chair in the lethargic hospital waiting room.

It would be a validation of sorts.

I try and imagine the untrammelled space I will leave,
fluid and deep-sea'd, nebulous and shape-shifting.
Yet perhaps that's not how others remember us
preferring to recall the solid and tangible
something to be rebuked, or stroked, or prodded, or loved.
If you could take this insubstantial past-promise of me

might you explore the sense of those rare words, to see
if contact with my roughly chiselled
and hand-sewn pin-bled phrases touched you?

It could be a validation of sorts.

C ongregation at a Twitcher's Sunset

"They beat out rhythmic drum solos on hollow trees.
They watch me, watching them.
They watch me as spies would, always out of reach.

"Some bring gifts.
Gift-giving is their natural encore
        placing them where they can't be missed.
By my bed, a small wooden box,
        each compartment guarding treasure:
        a gold bead, a pearl earring,
        a quartz crystal, a red Lego brick."

He comes to understand the purpose of meaningful sounds,
        understands a culture of tool-making is important,
        that complicated societies are the real spur
        for making informed decisions.
All too late, he discovers
        an uncanny ability to distinguish expressions,
        the alphabet, paintings by Monet and Picasso.

He yearns for his home and treasures
        during an illness long and drawn out.
Hard-wiring underlies memory and decision-making;
        his own is flawed, fraying, fragile.

They watch him as spies would,
        already decked out in their mourning dress.

G as Street Basin

Forty years   misplaced.
Brushed aside
        like Stuart's glasses branch-snagged
        casually flipped slow-motion
        into canal-dark water at the last-morning tiller
        between here and somewhere else.

Years dissolving   inexplicably
as a gentle wake
        resolves back into nothing but a ripple
        the tried and tested ruse
        of leaving not a trace of our recent passing
        for the silent boats that follow.

In harsh shadows   ghostly
memories dance;
        memories of mooring ropes and narrow bunks
        and pubs now driven from soft focus
        into something they didn't used to be
        trapped in their own navigation.

Barley wine.   Skittles.
Courses charted.
        Uncertain fragments wistfully recalled
        as the unexpected bequest of an unplanned stroll,
        spectres on the Gas Street towpath
        after all these rapidly accelerating years.

They see their town slipping into decline;
the hospital on the brink of bankruptcy,
a shopping mall closing.
Not renowned for metaphors,
economists are recording 'deaths of despair'.

Confronting the erosion of their majority status
is an unresolvable problem for people
who built something from the ground up,
who yearn for a repeat of their treasured history
like a cable re-run of a forties' black-and-white movie.

Vulnerable, wowed by the theatrical,
they succumb to mirrors and smoking dry-ice,
to polo shirts, and khaki stepping out of the shadows -
the neighbourhood normal, gun-toting from the saddle
of a re-sprayed carousel stallion.

To protect themselves from a lack of bias,
these new veterans cite research that distills
their problem into a few vacuous words
which they bow-wrap and hand out,
the illusion of gifting something tangible.

The peril of language is our weakness,
as potent as shaking a fist at a thunder cloud.
And all the while the soundbite marches on,
stories spiral forward propelled by their own weight,
and sanity dances towards the edge of the precipice.

Untitled haiku

a few precious words
are released unprotected
into the maelstrom

living on their wits
and the genius to melt
into an image

trick of the mind's eye
to trace pattern myth and ghosts
in the never-there

when we caress them
our crass manipulation
falls so often short

yet there they remain
imperious and perfect
our slaves and masters

Fossil-hunting

We travel down a gravel road to a broken bank
dust kicking up from the skidding tyres
as they struggle for grip on a misjudged incline.

The backdrop is a panoply of greys.
Above the rough sea, the clouds push hard towards us,
White Horses fling their manes to the cold-washed beach.
The whistle of the wind, the crash of the waves,
a symphonic backing for the rough snarl
of the gravel-spewing tyres.

Imprinted in the scattered stone below, slight
after-images of an intricate shadow thrown decades ago.
Imagine a forest, late-day sun
slanting through unfamiliar foliage;
the smell of the forest floor, perhaps pine;
the sweetness of recent-crushed leaves;
the residue of fruits half-eaten by unseen beasts.
On a cold, grey, shingle beach
a stone tracing preserves that day,
the capture of an autumn afternoon.

Departing, imagine the wheel-spin
as we strive for grip on the broken bank,
our words disappearing, leaving no known descendants.

THE MYTHS OF
NATIVE TREES

A lder

we sought refuge
                    concealment
mistaken in our naïve belief
hiding beneath the alders' canopy
            our secret
                        our elopement
would remain hidden

away from the trail
the heavy ground slowed our escape
and later
            mired ankle-deep in water
we understood why some paths
                                    are seldom trodden

in a forest   green is no camouflage

A sh

"my passion is animals" you said
            your voice in mid-distance
                        off-hand
                as if it belonged somewhere else
                        to someone else

"the serpent and the eagle" you said
            after I queried your favourites
"they are full of insight and wisdom"
                your voice betraying a longing
                        for something mystical or magical
                                of another place

"did you know" you said
"from the antlers of a deer
sprang the rivers of the world?
that the serpent and the eagle
protect the purity of springs?"

     I was always confused in your world
          as if it were not my home

"you belong in the underworld" you nearly said
       watching me as I fashioned
       spears from the bough of an ash
          then concentrating
           took aim

C herry

in the tree
the cuckoo watches
as the bough
         bends
with a force it never knew it had
to kiss the hand of a woman
heavy with her own fruit

the bird has no song for this
and feels
      for the first time
an interloper

so silently it unfurls its feathers
and moves on

Scots Pine

there is a whisper in the air
       silence-pure
a mountain breeze caresses
attentive leaf-bound boughs
       swaying regally

picking a cone from the ground
you wonder aloud if they have always been there
these trees
       these cones

"if you take one home
does it open and close with time?"

obscurely
I am reminded of your heart
and love's inconstancy
and know I cannot answer

At 'Friar's Crag', Boxing Day, 2018

we saw the flowers first
tied hurriedly askew to a low fence
less fence than coarse attempt
to keep us to the rocky path
the path from where we saw the dust
not dust but pale grey ash
less scattered than smuggled
like an escape-tunnel digger's
tip-and-run under cover of night
their loved one reunited with a favoured haunt
a place where now they lie

unprotected from the elements
they once embraced
and to which they must finally succumb

the ash will be gone tomorrow
nothing left
but the flowers we saw first

R ailway Vignettes

1
sheep lie in a field
there   a black one
another   and again
the rogue family of the estate

across the frosted hedgerow
the scar of a cavernous hole
a burial mound inverted
and silent diggers poised
in their uniform yellow
waiting for the day to start
like sheep in a field

2
the guard announces Burton-on-Trent
in bouncing sing-song
as if it's Torremolinos or some chart-topping destination
to which all your tracks have been leading

it isn't of course
but rather a nondescript place
with areas of posh and not
and huge brewery funnels
pumping the aroma of beer
into clean spring air

3

she limps as she walks
not because her trolley bag
black and trailing behind her
like a vaguely disobedient dog
is especially heavy
nor because she is overweight (she is)
or her tights are laddered (they are)

she looks out of kilter
her hair uncombed   apologetic
as if it has already been a long day

she looks as if she wants
to be leaving   again
but she is just arriving
limping as she does

4

a woman sits with her son
and silently contemplates
the accidents of history
she wishes she could undo
as easily as slipping
a ring from a finger
as if that would free her
'til life us do part
free to go searching
for the things she lost
or the things she believes
have passed her by
like vignettes seen through
a railway carriage window

Protest

the banners were hand-made
crafted from garage leftovers
and worn out felt-tips   or their kids' ancient painting sets
letters shadowed in highlighter orange
          for emphasis   and fire
                    colours running in the rain
they stole incendiary chants from the terraces
recycled   repurposed

the uniformed looked on   passive
as if nothing to do with them
unconnected bystanders
out for a stroll with their mates
in kevlar   just in case

in the drizzle some heads were hot
blinded by their cause
shackled by the impotence of their words

an onlooker smoked languidly
and in a shop doorway a photographer
searched for an angle that would look perfect
in black-and-white
          waiting   in case it all kicked off

people moved slowly   or didn't move at all
tension taut like an elastic band
about   to   snap

a cry   the holding of breath
then from the back   an arm enflamed   swung

years later
the BBC voice-over has become legend
its words the narrative
        of the struggle
                the conflict
                        the outcome
and the black-and-white photo
of a uniform smeared with blood
            something motionless on the ground
                is fable
                        or the only truth

the following weekend in bright sunlight
'keepers in smart peaked caps   kits vibrant
the local derby a one-all draw
                        and the pubs all full again

 York Weekend
(with apologies to Philip Larkin)

The station spews them out
in lurid shades of orange, spray
tan-tottering towards Happy Hours
designed to last all day.

Over-stilettoed and
squeezed into unforgiving fabric
they crease and wobble into town
in search of something magic;

eyes Egyptian-painted
deifying inebriation,
steeped in alcohol inside-out
ripe for mummification.

Raw accents echo across a river
that embraces machismo revelling
and those trying to beat the odds
or land a touch on spread betting.

Later they will dribble
spent onto the Knavesmire,
a tattooed wave of humanity
in celebrity-copycat attire.

Betrayed by anti-climax,
staggering, they feint a clout,
piss in hedges, puke on lawns,
emptied by a great day out.

E rosion

the pebbled beach
a congregation celebrating
the tribulation of tides
smoothed to impossible ellipses
begging to be spun back out to sea
as if relaunched into their past

and I wonder how the tides have worked on you
corrupting your once unblemished surface
each wave-clash sending blade-sharp shards
dangerous through the air

what was it shaped you
to become the dark flint
firing sparks from our past

G rief

there is a space where you used to be

I see it on grey station platforms
and in shuffling supermarket aisles

strange how it is never occupied
                               despite the throng

I feel it during countryside walks
my hand abandoned
constantly surprised to find yours
                               not there

a voice   lost like me   asks
not why you are not here
                               but why am I

and why do I bother to make that journey
          or go to work
                    or read this book

they say all stories have two sides
if that is true
then I am living half of ours
staring at the space you once filled

L etting Go

an entrance through rough scrub
leads to unmapped landfill
poorly disguised behind forlorn hedgerows
scant welcoming for birds

rutted tracks betray the trespassers
who come in darkness
to divest themselves of the unwanted
sloughing off flakes of veneer
as if snakes shedding skin

my car steers erratically
its narrow wheelbase a mismatch
for deep and puddled ruts
its chassis gouging my progress
skimming the mud's crust
like a tell-tale tracing
on a well-worn map

parked beside a buckled mattress
I unload today's modest offering
      part-read classics
      the corpse of an unkept diary
      a notebook whose last few naked pages
         seem beyond salvation

tossing them into the blackness
should feel like a release
but they are greeted by silence
like sacrifices looking for a cause

Re-reading Larkin

All the while I can sense him
looking over my shoulder
as if marking my homework,
a dubious figure in a grubby raincoat
loitering at the back.
Is that expression the resentment
he has to loiter there at all

or merely suburban anger at time
wasted on me?

Annoyed at the intrusion
he tuts under his breath
as he might a noisy bookworm.

"How many more fucking times
do I need to tell you?"

Waving a stubby pencil at a half-rhyme
he shakes his head
then shoulders his camera
determined to capture more of this miserable life
before it gets too late.

Left alone,
I weigh-up the merits of pairing
'blarney' with 'money'
and ask myself why *I* like to go into churches.

S hrouded

in the gloom a headland bleeds to mist
colours running into grey
a wash as soft as any cheek-brushed kiss

a gull's abrasive scream
flies across the dunes then fades away
beckons to another yet unseen

scan the fluid shore for fractured clues
as each tide-tied pebble begs its say
in a puzzle dressed in camouflage fatigues

now beyond limp memory's fetch
and cloaked in out-of-focus overlay
history's fickle piper suggests a day

of breakers   sun-studded waves
a ballet of wind-blown marram swathes
and butterflies dancing in the vetch

H ide

Sleuth-like you scavenge for clues:
the roughness of bark to the touch,
a musky odour you can smell in the fog.

You imagine a slender, mouse-grey bird
and strive to describe it given only
the nocturnal song of one of its neighbours.

Undaunted, there is no option but
to go deeper in on a close summer night,
embracing a legend worth believing.

Absorbed in a cocoon of quiet industry
you find him watching and waiting,
perched in the blind, silently writing.

V ocal | Chords

I want a voice of my own. | A rasp like Dylan's - | two bars, you know it's him. | A voice is not what you say | but how you say it; | Dylan could wring agonies | from Mary and her little lamb. | If you spoke another language | you could still tell it was Dylan | or Sinatra. | Or Betjeman, come to that. | A voice exists beyond the words, | in the insubstantial spaces between them, | living the high-life in a parallel universe. | So I weave words on the page | to create a portal to another realm, | to connect to a sense beyond the surface, | braving all the self-scrutiny | to summon up the courage | to see if I can get there.

Pilgrimage

We set-off before first light
the pre-dawn drive straining the eye.
Numbed by pulsing headlights, my sight
tried to race ahead, to preview the majesty
of the village beneath the hill,
a return to a bygone age
where all we knew and loved remained there still.
It was a pilgrimage
even if we struggled in the car
and travelling wasted too much of the day.
"That's just the way things are"
you said. We were about halfway,
stopping for lunch at noon
already resigned to return too soon.

In Mourning

There used to be a sparkle in your eye
fired by a vigorous joust with life.
I watched it die
as I watched you lose your wife,
you so desperate to weep
dry-eyed at being left behind.

She would have told you what to do: to keep
focused on the future, your mind
alive, sharply honed on how to spend
your time, not waste it
as she feared she had at the end.

You say I cannot understand it,
how heavily it sits,
not death but the emptiness it commits.

THE HOMELESSNESS
OF A CHILD

E lm Grove Library

it sat back from the road   apologetically
barricaded by modest gardens and a low wall
a municipal bungalow
        the antithesis of splendour and promise

yet inside was a treasure trove
the spot the 'X' marked
yards of books on low-slung shelves
        child-high   alluring

feigning illness to bunk-off school again
the boy took possession
imagining a moat around 'A' to 'D'
then drawbridge up
honed-in on Blyton
                famous

                        secret

what seeds were sown then
not those of adventure
but saplings of a different kind
        of imagination
                of invention
of the power of putting one word in front of another
and seeing where they took you

The site of the library has long since been redeveloped into University student accommodation.

95

A lverstoke

elevated above the road
even the church excluded us
not that we were interested
        foreign to upbringings
        investing in such promises

walking round the lanes
peering through windows of shops never entered
feeling like outcasts or refugees
        as much without hope as without money
        or the right shoes

it formed a template
like a model village in which impossible people lived
something to aspire to
        a tattoo to be magicked into reality
        or a scab to be picked at

as if a commentary on his time there
after he left they condemned the school
its fabric unsafe
        turning the land to more profitable use
        and dreams to rubble

I n Stanley Park

at one point
a circular embrace of rhododendrons
branches conjoined into a single crown
and at their heart
a hollowed space
a secret den

where boughs grow horizontally
or have been cajoled there
persuaded into love seats

Linda sits
fiery blonde hair threatening orange
brown well-deep eyes
the lips he longs to kiss

eight feet is a chasm in this shady calm
the dried earth between them
                              quicksand
forbidding any move

but that is the man talking
the man who now knows time is precious
          and life passes as quickly as the voices
          that drifted in from the path nearby
who knows what it's like
          to hold someone close
          to feel the beating of their heart

it seems unfair
such wisdom was denied an eleven-year-old boy
who needed it then
so much more than the man does now

years later
he saw her in a supermarket car park
she was older
yet her hair still that burnished colour
and he dared to wonder
how life would have been lived
if a young boy had stood
and walked eight feet

For Liz

fifty years since

years smuggled illegally across the border
disguising themselves
       with incident   accident   crisis
and from nowhere I am reminded of
an effervescent girl
who laughed as if she were party to secrets
       kept from the rest of us
who courted scandal with short skirts
       the first to wear a bra
who took me to the park that sunny Saturday
       and introduced me to my first wet kiss

I have felt guilty all these years
for the way I cast you aside
a twelve-year-old's fear victorious over everything

how wistful is this
recognising at the other end of time
how much of life you owned
       and how much of it you offered me

Giro-scopic

once
when the Thursday Giro failed to arrive
not having the bus fare
they walked the four miles
to seek salvation in the drab social security office
taking a number
       sitting on harsh plastic chairs

waiting their turn

to beg

then unrewarded
to walk all the way back
those same four miles in reverse
her purse
        empty as promises

what did they talk about
all that way
                there and back

G ladys

You could have built walls from her cakes,
carved them into precisely defined slabs;
they were large, chocolatey and oddly grey
with the pitted consistency of breeze block.
Cutting the first slice after tea was a ritual,
a special treat for post-school Mondays.

In a house of twisted personalities
exaggerated by the mental shrapnel of war
her laugh was resistant to misery and disease,
a cackle that challenged you to defy it,
exploding to deafen the under-breath chunter
of a brother who'd lost more than weight in Burma.

I felt for Uncle George too, marooned like me,
as long-suffering as he was grey-topped tall,
handcuffed to a recurrent Poe-like nightmare
from which he could never escape -
or from which she would never release him.
I was too young then to decipher life.

One by one, death smuggled them away,
though only after I had been partially rescued.
Arthur's going finally ended his bitter war,
and not even her laugh could save George,
silently eaten away from the inside
all the while defending his back-bent dignity.

Suffering, punishment and freedom
I discovered later; a three-card-trick
played chest-close, ace hidden up the sleeve.
In a theatre beyond all vanquishing,
she rescued a child who loved her cakes
and who later missed the chance to thank her.

The Skip

rusting through paint-broken gaps
it juts into the road
hazardous on a blind bend
the only warning
     a badly-located orange cone
     its colour diluted by too much sun

the letters at its rim are flaked
inadequate clues
divulging nothing of purpose or ownership

curious
you look inside
     semi-guilty
afraid to be accused of scavenging for unworn-out things

in the abject and disorganised discard
     the odd flash of colour
          no more than heyday hints

there   a crushed box from a childhood toy
        the semi-hidden tangle of unattached wires
        the frame of something you cannot place
        the outline of a book
all are compromised
        like a puzzle with half the pieces thrown away

prompted
you remember the detritus in your pockets
        a used train ticket
        an old shopping list
        a pen dry of ink
you toss them furtive to the skip
where their landing makes no sound
        an accumulation instantly invisible

tomorrow
you will return
        to find the skip still there
        to add to the collection
the paint flaked a little more
        the hazard undiminished
                the story indecipherable

S idings

they arc from sight with bizarre elegance
an overgrown divergence
designated to home the unwanted   or the forgotten
weeds climb rusting axles
clogging memories of motion
and birds flit in the eerie silence
to reserve a first-class nesting site

The only reason

I wonder when certainty abandoned her

      as she walked towards the tube
           still cocooned by our brief farewell kiss

      or later   pulling pyjamas from a drawer
           in her studio flat

      or after days   or weeks   or years
           chiding herself for her foolishness

pyjamas would have suited her modesty
soft winceyette   pastel-coloured   subtly-patterned

she would have unbuttoned them slowly
as if each button were a step into the unknown
      a risk   a wager
and then taking my hand   trembling   into her own
placed it on a breast
      laying bare the truth kept hidden all those months
      just as she had whispered it when she left

      the only reason I'm not crying
      is because I know I'll see you again

Failures of Crimping

at the edges
attempts at precision
indentations aspiring to perfection
ambition blind-baked
against the inevitable corruption of heat

watching the clock count down
recall the flour-dusting of language
how we cajoled   pressed one word against another
striving for a recipe
to seal in the contents

hopeful and oven-gloved
we rescue our creation from the furnace
only to be dismayed by the insipid colour
the crust's crumbling
meaning calcified on the oven's floor

V ariations

(i)

Elgar plays "The Enigma" on spoons rescued from Geller
hammered straight by an amateur blacksmith
with a passion for buxom sopranos

if the notes are a little wayward
you forgive them given you can later eat trifle
with the instruments of their making

I'd like to see you do that with a cello
someone says stifling a laugh
and you wonder if they've been at the sherry
if it were an audition Elgar would have failed
no credit given for composition or commitment
nor the imaginative use of second-hand cutlery

(ii)

a hangover shaped the clock-face that way
sliding off the table   a metaphor for a mind
     struggling to keep a hold on things

he twirls unevenly curled moustaches
consolation in knowing reputation
     demotes incompetence before intent

yet there's something alluring about
bold unsophisticated colours   their sharp contrast
     both a promise and a threat

and from somewhere a melody he can't quite place
as if a string is untuned   or someone
     has bent a hammer in a baby grand

(iii)

he had begged a smile but had to settle for less
his best jokes betraying him
     and even arriving at one sitting cross-gartered
     failed to generate a spark

knowing the end-product would be inadequate
he resorted to amusing himself
     by bending tricks of draughtsmanship
     to enigmatic sleight-of-hand

it was all frustratingly amateurish of course
sacrificing time for the merely commercial
     a portrait of the ungrateful wife
     of a semi-important merchant

(iv)

his ally
hammered home the message
about stripping back
his unforgiving pencil attacking words
        its marks locusts in a feeding frenzy

a shallow drawer
became hospice for the vanquished
rescue of what had been lost
less for his own benefit
        than posterity's sanity

England his elopement
proved no wasteland at all
his dowry a gifting of place into legend
like variations whose first notes everybody knows
        no matter how badly they are played

(v)

if his own family had betrayed him like that
he would have taken a different line
an abdication less likely to backfire

still
it was cathartic to work things through
according to another's interpretation

profitable too

the irony hadn't escaped him
falling into fortune by mistake
a seed fertilised in an idle moment
        more luck than calling

never short of material
his rhythms mimic'd the people he knew
recycling old stories with a new twist
grateful his children had never bequeathed him a plot-line

except once

the ghost that haunted him

S hall We Dance

woken this morning by two pigeons
tap-dancing on the dormer ridge tiles
Astaire and Rogers honing a routine

pirouetting
she was lighter on her feet
weaving slender wing-arcs through the air
with an imaginary boa
while he   feathers on the tuxedo-side of grey
circled clumsily cooing *look at me*
as if discovering something for the first time

just like a man

beneath millions of roofs
dances of indeterminate duration
played out against the backdrop of office or kitchen
        garden or shed
        lounge or library
                    or bedroom
screenplays varying only in context
nuanced for circumstance
or clumsily rehashed like repeats
on a bargain-basement channel

episodes that blend into one
where the ending is given away in the opening credits
tentatively I begin my own dance once again
striving for invention and finesse
my shoes black-polished to within an inch of their lives
my dress-shirt white beyond white
my bow impeccably tied
and as I weave and circle feigning competence
my partner   who is all words   laughs

striving for an American Smooth or Argentine Tango
all I manage is a ham-fisted Conga
stumbling across the page
          tripping on the metre
                    misplacing a comma

A fter-words

then your words came tumbling out
like a river in full spate
a waterfall driving down into a pool
carved deep by the force of their syllables
and though you sat at its edge
playing the part of a detached observer
admiring the landscape   the picturesqueness of it all
there was no escaping the spray
rising like a mist
as if the words had broken on impact
and re-formed into something else
undeniable   unavoidable
and when you stood to go
unsure if you were glad to be leaving or not
you found that you were drenched
the remnants of words
permeating the surface of your skin

Quieted

one day it will be too late
and all those things I should have said
or wanted to say
will be lost
because I will not be here to say them
nor remember they needed to be said
in the first place

The Cricket

In mis-matched mugs, tea
- too weak, too strong -
sits alongside crumb-dusted plates
cradling the remnants of tradition:
sandwiches, cake, the sausage rolls
for which they had all headed
the locusts of the Away-team.
Reputations are made in the pavilion
rather than on the field of play,
yorkers and cover-drives bowled over
by the untainted reputation
of Madge's Victoria Sponge.
They still speak in hushed tones
of the weekend it was made by someone else.

Dissecting the first innings
men in whites
take conversational guard from personal perspectives
volume and chattiness correlating to wickets and runs
except for their ex-star pace-man who plays on past reputation
and is simply glad to be there
gifted a ham salad and a handful of crisps.

Second-sensing the clock
the Openers rise and return their empties
to the hatch beyond which wives
- engaged in entirely different confrontations -
wash and wipe,
compare flamboyant notes on children's progress,
exaggerated plans for holidays.
The Number Three follows after a respectful pause
leaving the Next-Man-In the age-old dilemma
as to when he should pad-up:
too early shows lack of confidence,
too late, he might be caught out.
The opposition watch for him to move,
looking for clues as to their chances
of defending one-six-three for eight.
Then the cacophony of spikes on the pavilion steps,
the ritual of umpires donning coats and counting stones,
fielders' practice-catching - the mirage of professionalism -
before they all head out to the square
like a flotilla of small boats on a rescue mission.

To save what, the match?
To celebrate the sanctity of Madge's Victoria
and the efforts of all the ladies?
To provide an environment for kids
to play at being Daddy
and butcher that late cut for which he longs to be famous?

No.
Against dwindling interest
and the lure of the electronic
this is about the preservation of England,
and when the umpire calls "play"
they know they are safe for another week at least.

The New-Build

"Make thee an ark of gopher wood; rooms shalt thou make in the ark, and shalt pitch it within and without with pitch." - Genesis 6:14

If it's not one thing it's another
his wife's favourite maxim
designed to cover every eventuality.
At the small formica table she kneads dough,
bemoans their moving from the city,
ties herself up in the knots of her past life,
the life before him.
It never rained until I met you
a contestable complaint.

He wades through omnipresent mud
to a makeshift garden office
- a windowless Portakabin with limited ventilation -
and questions inadequate plans,
listens to rain thrumming on the roof,
antics of cooped-up caravan-children,
the restlessness of animals
corralled outside.

This is not the future he was sold.

Rumour runs in rivulets;
whispers say it's the same everywhere,
banks bursting onto non-existent floodplains
where families like his sit and wait
uninsured against An Act of God.

Either side of the Gutter

Framed by walls of utilitarian brick
they sit on plastic chairs outside the Working Men's Club
and smoke, bemoaning traffic clogging the arterial junction,
diesels born from the privilege of a city regeneration programme.
Hacking unfiltered-Capstan coughs
they reminisce about the Old Days of sometime-jobs
and swap stories of bosses and foremen
every noun prefixed with their favourite adjective,
a word become second-nature and
particularly suitable in these dark days
of Eastern European 'invasion'.
And so they relished the chance to have their say,
basing their vote on a past that never existed
and the fact that Nigel Whatsisname likes a pint.

Later
unsettled dust gives them cause
to complain about pensions and the price of fags,
narratives informed by Red Top editorials
scanned only when they make it beyond
the inflated assets of page three.

You could have been like that
biased toward a father's genes
more out of work than in,
addicted to cigarettes and traps two and six
in the first race at Hackney,
Saturday morning's High Church.
Instead, you sit waiting at the lights
outside the Working Men's Club,
air-conditioned in your Audi,
bemoaning from an alternative viewpoint
fucking Brexit.

The Judgement

"If I mistook my literary escapades
for legitimate adventures in the belly of the beast
do not misread them as premeditated follies
but rather the innocent output of the ham-fisted."

An honest confession or some linguistic sleight-of-hand designed to throw us off the scent, whining and wheedling, aiming to be gifted absolution or excuse unquenchable addiction?

Hidden away in some spine-broken notebook, exhibits we suspect he would prefer not held to the light; their irregular warp and weft and a certain looseness in the fabric, exposure he is keen to avoid.

In a rudimentary image crudely drawn, one such offering presents - in the middle of a pedestrian bridge - an iron gate padlock-shut, its key long since slipped through a trouser-pocket hole, gutter-fallen and kicked unknowingly toward the oblivion of the drains. Soaked by rain and decomposing autumn leaves, it wallows in an overcoat of mud while he stands pretentiously examining the gate, cold ungloved hands rattling the frame, hoping for hinges to give way under the modesty of his onslaught. He envies the greenness on the gate's other side as if there were a better rainbow to which he could upgrade.

All superstitious nonsense.

Rain chafes as hard on that side as this, the wind's howling unmoderated; yet in its whistling he pretends to messages.

"If it is a crime to have tried to depict a fraction of things seen or felt
then I plead guilty, beg the sentence be not harsh,
and ask consideration be given in recognition of a good war waged."

"Pathetic pleadings; as if they could educate the margins in a reputable court of law!"

"So it is a trial then; guilty until proven innocent.
There are circumstances to be considered in my defence;
'contributing factors'."

"Such as?"

"As a child, teachers who would
resort to the slipper for extra-curricular learning;
times' tables written out on blackboards,
and spellings tested weekly!
Isn't that torture worthy of something?
And bread, hard on the second day, off by the third.
Now it lasts forever, hormone-injected,
protected in American-style freezers.
Or gears on buses that ground when they changed;
and spinning the handle on shoulder-slung machines,
conductors dispensing flimsy tickets.
There was always paper, and carbon copies;
library books with pasted labels, columns for stamps
thumped down as you left the building,
reading permission slips.
We played football in the unforgiving street;
spent all our pocket money in funfair slots;
chased girls hopelessly, never catching one
- especially later in our Saturday-night Travolta-failings.
We chanted on terraces and threw up
in the backs of friends' cars
after three-too-many pints;
we scrabbled for meaning in the fog of growing up
always assuming we had it grasped
before it slipped through our fingers.
Surely all that experience is worth something?"

The judge - a spitting image of the defendant - dons a black cape to
pass sentence; "Life" the inevitable consequence.

PREVIOUSLY
UNPUBLISHED

The old life

in almost every kind of light
his forearms mimic
the skin of a snake about to slough
or a paper-bag used too many times
wrinkle-thin
about to crack
                    wide open

yet
it teases at a capacity for something else
as if waiting to be filled

with what

all that's left are memories

        of the cross-court forehand winners
        played on ice-pocked university courts

        that one majestic in-swinger
        pilfering the off-stump bail
        like a slick-fingered thief

        of wrapping her in an embrace
        he thought would never end

in the darkness
he dreams those things again
almost as if the skin had split
and released him
                    back into a life once loved

The Gourmands

on a Freetown city-centre market stall
like undertakers waiting for business
two vultures perch funereally
and gaze on well-intentioned white flesh

the birds sharpen their talons

unfurling a wing in readiness
for an hors d'œuvres at least
one incants the names of entrées
from its favourite recipe book

*thigh cutlet coated with mango jus
soft and tender*

      light on the mango says the other

*ribs with plantain
roasted sweet on a brazier*

*calves in groundnut stew or
shoulder wrapped in banana leaves*

tendons braised in tarragon

*fricassee of fingers
served with okra*

pan fried patella

ground groin

*and even though it can be a little on the fatty side
grilled steaks of gluteus maximus
studded with cloves*

picking up on the theme
the second vulture proposes
a more simple menu

liver   *raw*
kidney   *raw*
heart   *raw*
                    and only just stopped beating
ears
eyes
spleen
testicles

au poivre? suggests the first

       raw

your problem is that you've got no taste
says the first vulture
before it stretches away
to offer its black silhouette to the sky

Drawing Breath at the National Trust

Her voice carries.

No full stops
she is all conjunctions:
'but' and 'so' and 'yet' and 'and'.
Years of catching up to do
chasing herself through unpunctuated sentences.
And after, the crows come to pick at crumbs
from the cheese scone taken an age to eat,
minor mouthfuls when she paused
offering hair-line cracks for her companion's
feeble wedge of unfinished phrases.

When she has finally been overwhelmed
the crows will still be there
dropping into the silent full stop
of her no longer drawing breath.

M y skin

reminds me of someone else

surely not there all those yesterdays ago
patterns of freckles on my upper arms
like jewels from a heist   or spies
smuggled in under cover of darkness
camouflaged in a well-used safe house

or perhaps
they are paying homage
an inadequate tracing from the template of another
gifted or taken surreptitiously
under a different kind of cover
      if so
      then I cannot recall the body
      to which the skin belonged

or yet again
perhaps they are a chart
subtle constellations by which
one might navigate the darkness
      but how inconvenient that would be
      forced to make yourself naked
      to know in which direction to travel

S hadows

1

doused in the acid glow of streetlights
you walk hospital-bound
tortured by the threat of halogen

your shadow mocks
as it rotates silently about you
ahead   behind
never one thing or the other
an inconsistent joke with unsubstantial punchlines

Payne's-grey edges chamfer to smoothness
an aura that could be anyone's
a stalker superglued to your feet
less-than-secret agents mimicking your every move
whilst elsewhere   cowering in a darkened corner
that unembellished part of you
(the more honest part some might say)
keeps its head down
waiting for the lights to go out

2

when you were a child you would run and jump
trying to catch your shadow out   to land on yourself

it was easier chasing after unsuspecting others
who never felt the impact

of small shoes flatfoot-slapping on pavements
your father assuming you were dodging the cracks

because that was what all children did
the game you played   even when you weren't playing

3

against an LED-backdrop
and the fragile metronome of a heart-rate monitor
he lies and waits
patience disguised as sleep

eyes closed he imitates death
as best he can
like trying on an expensive coat for size
before the debit card comes out

he wonders if the little things
will be missed most of all
even knowing he will not be there
to miss them

the images that bait him
are x-ray crisp
pixels of silver-grey on laminate so shiny
you think they might slip off

onto the floor goes his diaphragm
his heart   his lungs
and with those the smoky clouds of his days
good riddance to bad rubbish

4

when dawn comes
streetlights abandon the world

his memory fades as
the child skips away

the metronome is silent
and the shadows win again

On Walking Boots

i.m. Elizabeth Barraclough

The snow was horizontal that Spring
marching up Walla Crag in her wake
me wondering if the walk had been a big mistake.
Eventually, crying from the blizzard's sting
we found the crest, looked through the rage
of a white-out over Derwent
Water, then began our perilous descent.

Was it a kind of test? A rite of passage?
Her validating I was worthy?
It became a trial that felt boundless
always wanting to do more to impress,
to earn an honour from her sovereignty.

Now she is no longer here I'll never know
if I passed muster in the snow.

Examination

*"you should express your answer
in relation to a single variable"*

or   from a position of profound uncertainty
uncover a secret both full and devoid of meaning

against the absence of background chatter
we strive for clarity
keen to do as we're told
and show our workings in the margins

"calculators are not allowed"

become a stub
the pencil slips from our grasp
and falling to the floor
finds a crack in the boards

tied to decisions already made
we mourn its loss
as if truth had escaped with it

"this question is worth five marks"

bullied by the tick of an insistent metronome
we examine the box where we wrote

$$x = 42$$

and hope that's close enough

"do not leave the room until your time has elapsed"

Acknowledgements

A very small number of these poems are 'semi-found' pieces, based on material already existing in the public domain e.g. museum catalogues, magazine articles. In all of these cases, reference to the original sources has, unfortunately, long been lost.

Nevertheless, I remain indebted to the authors of those artefacts - whether public institutions, fellow writers, museum and gallery curators etc. - and am grateful for their unwitting but invaluable contributions without which some of these poems would not exist in their current format.

Note: It is entirely likely that, at some point in the future, the poems in the final section - 'Previously Unpublished' - may be combined with other new work to form a new collection.

Lightning Source UK Ltd.
Milton Keynes UK
UKHW040739160223
417122UK00003B/479